Sugne

ACKNOWLEDGMENTS

For their generous help, we would like to thank Deborah S. Jones, Larry B. Bilbrough, and Curtis M. Graves of NASA Headquarters. Our warm thanks go also to Dr. Harry Herzer III and Dr. Bevan M. French of NASA for their thoughtful review of the manuscript and to Corwith Hansen and Martha Bell for their patience.

Photographs and artwork courtesy of NASA with the following exceptions: Photograph on page 30 and illustrations on pages 12, 13, 14, 15, 27, 28, 39, and 41 by Don Dixon. Copyright © 1974, 1975, 1976, 1981, 1983, 1985 by Don Dixon. Charts and diagrams on pages 8–9, 19, 20, 23, and 41 by Brian Sullivan. Copyright © 1985 by Brian Sullivan.

For my mother
—R.L.H.

The first one, for Victoria
—R.A.B.

SIMON & SCHUSTER BOOKS FOR YOUNG READERS
An imprint of Simon & Schuster Children's Publishing Division
1230 Avenue of the Americas, New York, New York 10020

15   14

Library of Congress Cataloging-in-Publication Data

Hansen, Rosanna.   My first book of space.

"Developed in conjunction with NASA."
Summary: Introduces the solar system, examines each planet, and looks at the stars of space.
1. Astronomy—Juvenile literature. 2. Planets—Juvenile literature. [1. Astronomy. 2. Planets] I. Bell Robert A.
II. Sullivan, Brian, ill. III. Dixon, Don ill. IV. United States. National Aeronautics and Space Administration. V. Title.
QB46.H18   1985   523.2   85-13131

ISBN 0-671-60262-4

Cover photo: Saturn as photographed by Voyager. The colors of the photo have been enhanced to bring out details.
Cover designed by Antler & Baldwin, Inc.

My First Book of Space

DEVELOPED IN CONJUNCTION WITH NASA

BY ROSANNA HANSEN
AND ROBERT A. BELL

Simon & Schuster Books for Young Readers

This is how our planet Earth looks from a spaceship. It floats in space like a beautiful blue marble, covered with swirling white clouds. Underneath the clouds, you can see the blue oceans and brown land. You can also see the large patch of white covering the bottom of Earth. That white patch is the snow and ice of the South Pole.

Millions of miles from Earth is the mighty sun, the center of our solar system. Earth is one of nine planets that travel around the sun. The planet closest to the sun is Mercury. Then come Venus, Earth, Mars, Jupiter, Saturn, Uranus, Neptune, and Pluto. In the picture on the next page, you can see all the planets and their paths around the sun.

NASA

(above) Astronaut Eugene Cernan, commander of the Apollo 17 moon mission, standing on the dusty surface of the moon. Notice the footprints made by his boots.

◀ *This photograph of Earth was taken by astronauts traveling to the moon in the Apollo 17 spacecraft.*

The Solar System

The sun is the biggest and heaviest body in our solar system. It is much bigger than any of the planets. If the sun were the size of a basketball, Earth would only be as big as a dried pea, Jupiter as big as a peach, and Pluto as big as a grain of sand. This picture doesn't show you the true size of the planets compared to the sun. If it did, most of the planets would be too small for you to see.

The planets travel around the sun in special paths called orbits. This picture shows you where the orbits are, but you can't really see them in space. While the planets travel around the sun, they also move in another way. They spin around and around like giant tops.

Seven of the planets have moons that circle around them. Earth has one moon, which you can often see at night. Saturn has the most moons of any planet—at least 22 of them.

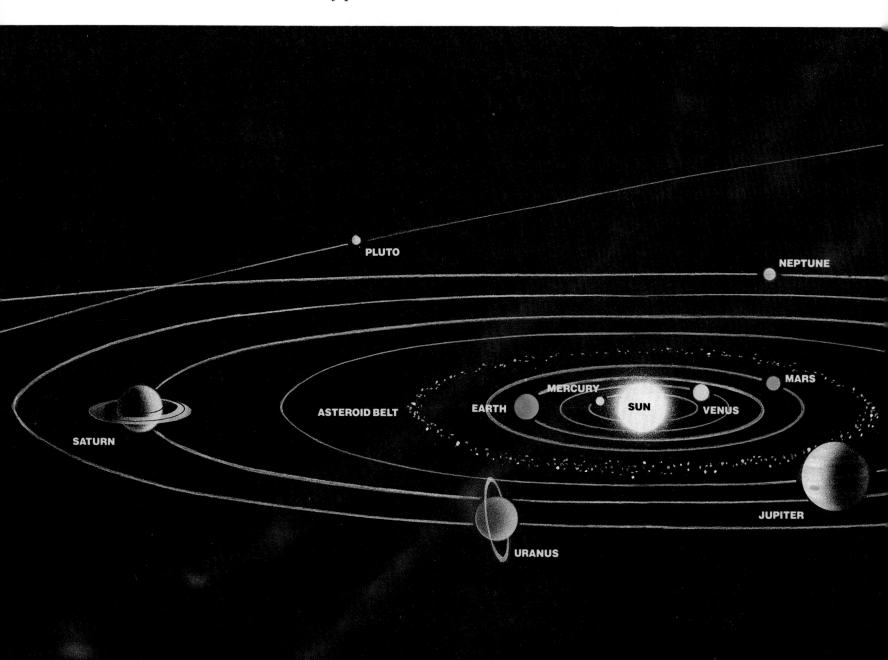

PLUTO

NEPTUNE

MARS

MERCURY

ASTEROID BELT   EARTH   SUN   VENUS

SATURN

JUPITER

URANUS

Meteoroids are part of the solar system, too. So are asteroids and comets. Meteoroids are chunks of rock that move through space. Most of them are very small. Asteroids are bigger chunks of rock, metal, and ice. Thousands of them travel around the sun in an orbit between Mars and Jupiter. Comets are balls of frozen gas and rock. Sometimes they are called "dirty snowballs."

Our solar system has many things in it—the sun, planets, moons, meteoroids, comets, and asteroids. But the sun is the biggest and the most important part of all.

A Force Called Gravity

What makes the planets orbit the sun? Why don't they fly off into space?

The planets keep moving around the sun because of the force called gravity. Everything in the solar system has gravity. Everything pulls at everything else. The bigger an object is, the more gravity it has and the harder it pulls at other things.

The sun is the biggest object in the solar system, so it has the strongest pull of all. Its gravity tugs hard at the planets and keeps them from flying off into space.

This picture shows you how the sun's gravity holds the planets in their orbits. The boy has a ball on a string that he is whirling around his head. The string acts like the sun's gravity. It holds onto the ball and keeps it from flying out into space. So the ball keeps moving around and around in its orbit. The planets move around the sun in much the same way.

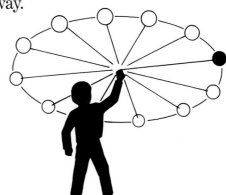

The Sun

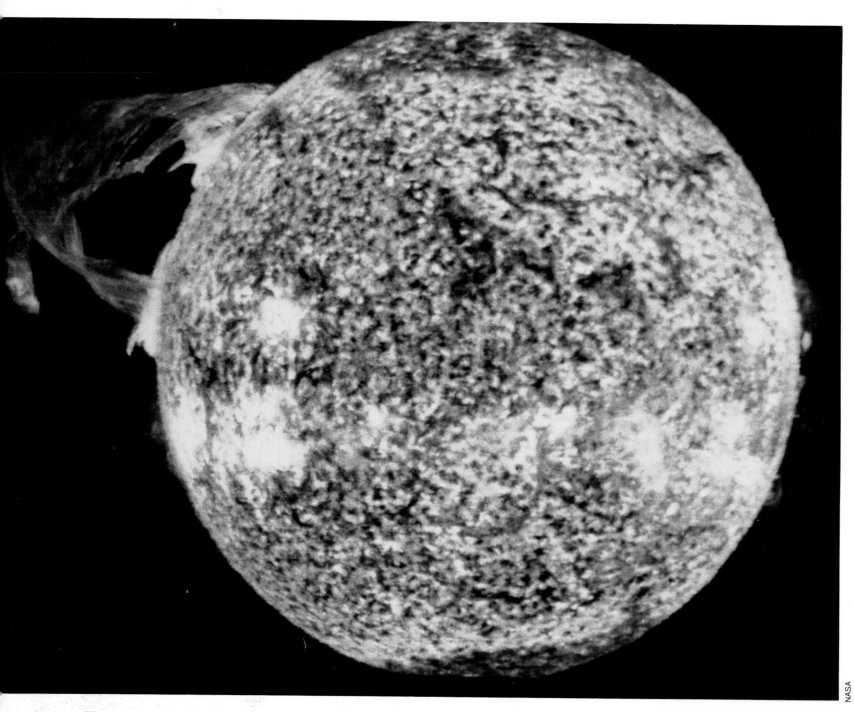

The sun as photographed from the space station Skylab. The huge tongue of gas exploding from the sun is called a prominence.

The sun is a star—the only star in our solar system. Since it is the star nearest to us, it looks much bigger and brighter than the other stars we see at night.

Like all stars, the sun is a huge ball of hot, glowing gases. The gases in the sun are so hot that they blaze with a fierce, brilliant light. The light shines so brightly that we can't look straight at the sun without hurting our eyes. (*Never look directly at the sun—not even for a second. If you do, you may hurt your eyes very badly.*)

The sun is 93 million miles (150 million kilometers) from Earth. If we were on a spaceship that could fly from Earth to the moon in two days, it would still take us almost a year to fly close to the sun. As we flew nearer, we could see how huge the sun really is. More than one million planets the size of Earth could fit inside the sun—and there would still be lots of room to spare!

The sun looks like a raging, boiling ball of flame. The hot gases on its surface bubble and spin. They are never still. Sometimes a huge tongue of gas shoots out from the surface. These long tongues of gas are called prominences. The prominence shown in the picture at the left is about 367,000 miles (588,000 kilometers) long. (If you wanted to travel 367,000 miles on Earth, you could go around the middle of our planet almost 15 times.)

The sun's outer atmosphere, or corona, reaches into space for millions of miles. Scientists took this special photograph to study the corona. They blocked out the center of the sun and used several colors to show the corona's different parts.

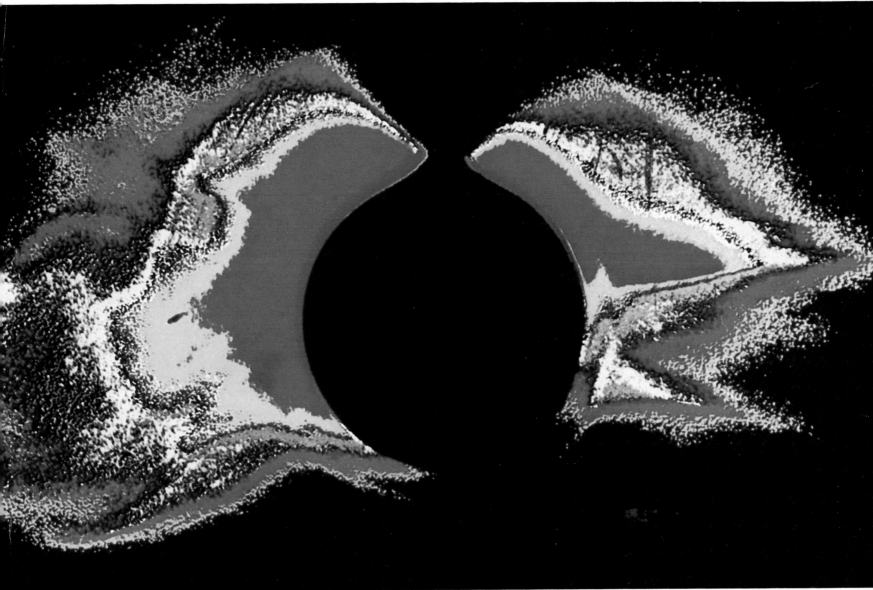

The hottest part of the sun is its center, or core. The core is like a giant nuclear furnace, where the temperature is about 25 million degrees Fahrenheit (14 million degrees Celsius). Energy pours up from the sun's core to its surface. Then it rushes out into space as waves of light. In about eight minutes and 20 seconds, the waves of light travel all the way through space to reach our planet Earth. That's much faster than any spaceship can travel.

Dixon

Birth of the Sun

Most scientists think that the sun began as a huge whirling cloud of dust and gas. About five billion years ago, the huge cloud slowly began to flatten out. Most of the cloud's gas and dust started to clump together into a gigantic, fiery ball.

Gravity squeezed the huge cloud so tightly together that it became hotter and hotter. It started to glow with tremendous heat. Finally, it grew so hot that it became a star.

While the star was forming at the center of the cloud, smaller clumps of gas were forming at other places in the cloud. These smaller clumps became the nine planets and their moons.

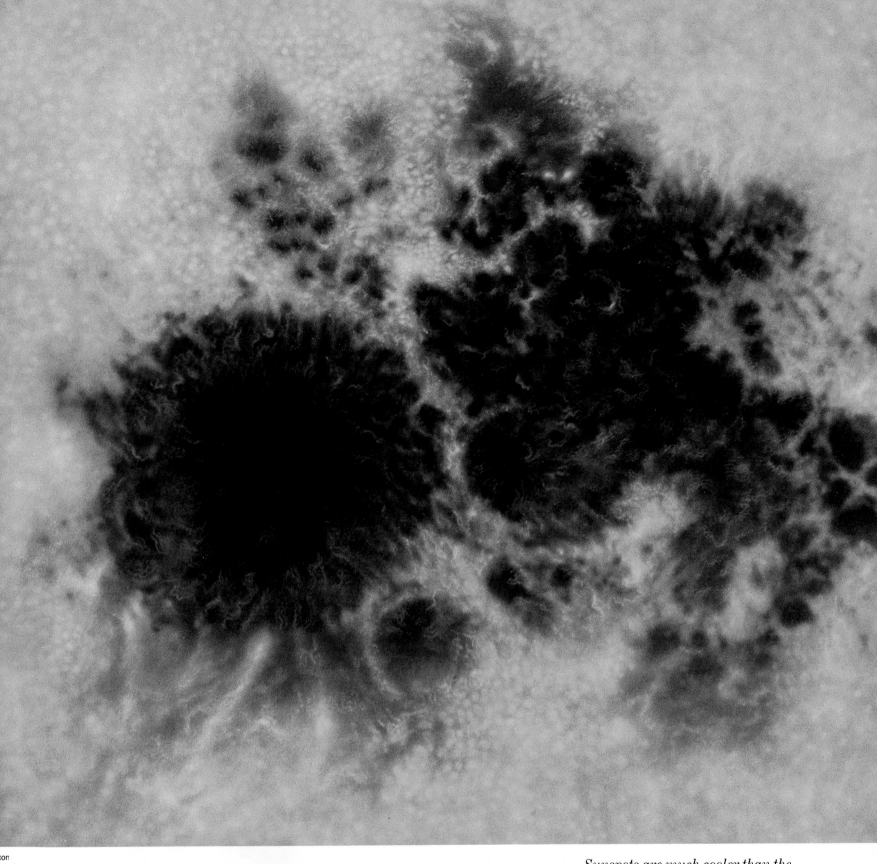

Scientists want to learn more about the sun, so they study it with telescopes and other instruments. Sometimes they see dark patches on the sun's face. These patches are called sunspots, and they look a little like gigantic freckles. Many sunspots are bigger than our entire planet. The sunspots may last for weeks or even months. Then they slowly fade away and disappear.

Our next stop is Mercury, the sun's closest neighbor. Mercury is only 36 million miles (58 million kilometers) from the sun, which is not a very big distance in space.

Sunspots are much cooler than the rest of the sun and don't shine as brightly. They look like dark patches on the sun's bright surface.

Mercury

Mercury is the planet closest to the sun. It is less than half the size of Earth. Mercury is also the speediest planet in the solar system. It circles the sun in only 88 Earth days, traveling at about one and a half times the speed of Earth.

Mercury is a small, rocky planet that is very much like our moon.

Dix

Dixon

Sunrise over Mercury's rocky desert. Because Mercury is so close to the sun, the sun looks much bigger and brighter in Mercury's sky than it looks on Earth.

While it travels around the sun, Mercury spins like a top. If you pushed a stick through a ball of clay and twirled the stick, the ball would spin around and around. That is how Mercury moves. It spins around an imaginary line that runs through its center. We call this imaginary line Mercury's axis. Each of the nine planets spins around on its own axis.

Mercury spins on its axis so slowly that one day on Mercury would last 59 days on Earth. A year on Mercury only lasts 88 Earth days, so this planet's day is almost as long as its year.

Mercury's surface is a rocky desert covered with billions of round holes called craters. The biggest crater, Caloris Basin, is a huge pit more than 800 miles (1,300 kilometers) wide. Mercury's craters make it look very much like our moon.

The sun looks nine times bigger from Mercury than it does from Earth. That's because Mercury is so close to the sun. The side of Mercury facing the sun has temperatures that soar to 873 degrees F. (467 degrees C.). That temperature is high enough to melt lead. On the side of Mercury away from the sun, the temperature plunges to −360 degrees F. (−218 degrees C.). No place on Earth gets even half as cold as that.

Mercury is hard to see from Earth because it is so small and so close to the sun. At certain times of year, it can be seen just after sunset or before sunrise. The rest of the time it is lost in the sun's glare.

Billions of years ago, Mercury had a layer of gases around it. But the gases slowly boiled away in Mercury's terrible heat. Today Mercury is a silent, dead world, broiling under the enormous sun.

Venus

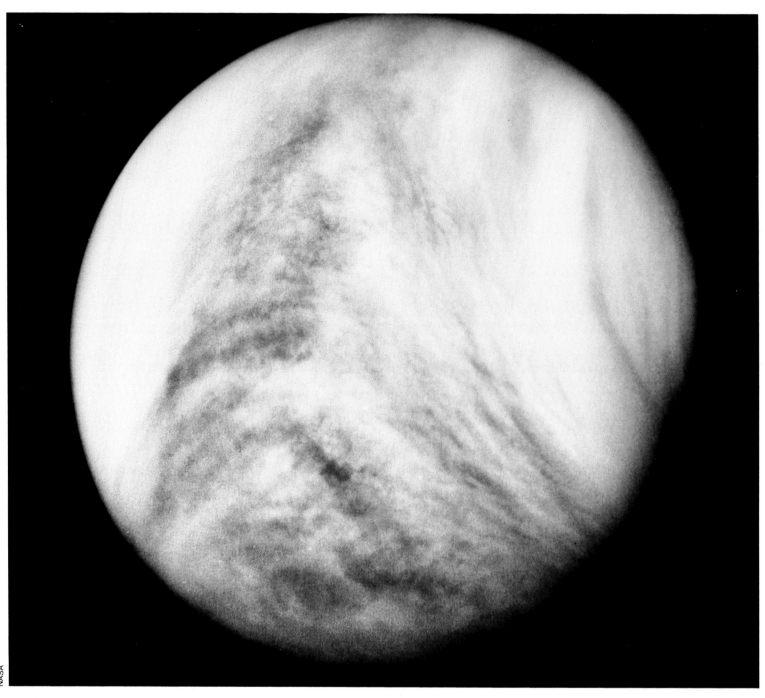

Venus as seen from the spacecraft Pioneer.

Next we come to Venus, the second planet in the solar system. Venus is almost as large as Earth. It is a beautiful world when you see it from space. It is wrapped in bright clouds. Venus is so beautiful that it was named for the Roman goddess of love and beauty.

Venus shines more brightly in the night sky than anything except Earth's moon. You can usually see it in the sky near the spot where the sun has just set. On Earth, we also call Venus the "evening star," because it looks like the first star of the night.

For a long time, scientists called Venus "Earth's twin." They hoped that the thick clouds of Venus hid a beautiful world below. Maybe there were strange plants and animals living on Venus—perhaps even people like ourselves.

We know now that Venus is nothing like Earth. The air of Venus would poison us. The land is mostly rocky desert with some high mountains and deep valleys. One mountain, called Maxwell Montes, is seven miles (11 kilometers) high. But there are no oceans, lakes, or rivers—no liquid water at all.

Venus circles the sun once in 225 Earth days. That makes it the second-fastest planet in the solar system. But Venus turns very slowly on its axis. A day on Venus lasts 243 Earth days.

If you stood on Venus's surface and looked up, the cloudy sky would be red. The clouds are so thick that little or no light reaches the surface. But the sun's heat does get through the clouds—and the clouds hold it in. The surface of Venus is almost 900 degrees F. (480 degrees C.). That's more than four times hotter than boiling water and hot enough to melt lead.

We have found no signs of life on Venus. There are certainly no people like us. Still, Venus could be a beautiful place to visit—as long as we could look at it from out in space.

This is how the surface of Venus may look. Maxwell Montes, the highest point on Venus, is on the right-hand side of this huge plain.

Earth

Earth is about 93 million miles (150 million kilometers) from the sun, and that is a good place for a planet to be. If the sun were closer, Earth would be terribly hot. If the sun were much farther away, Earth would be a dark, frozen world. The sun is the right distance from Earth for our kind of life.

We need warmth, air, water, and energy to live. Earth provides us with all these things. As far as we know, Earth is the only planet in the solar system that has plants, animals, and people living on it.

Earth rising over the surface of the moon. Half of Earth is shining in the sun's light and the other half is in darkness.

NASA

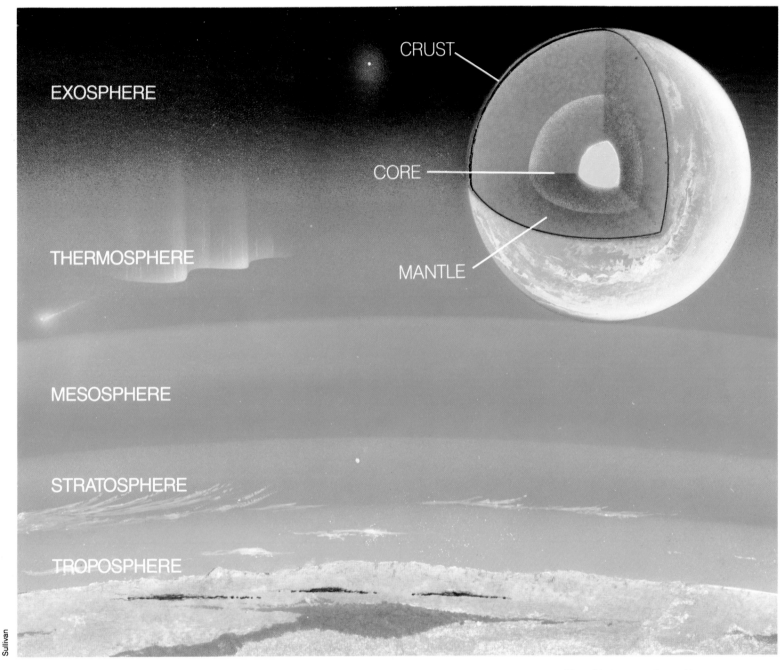

EXOSPHERE

THERMOSPHERE

MESOSPHERE

STRATOSPHERE

TROPOSPHERE

CRUST

CORE

MANTLE

Sullivan

Earth is a giant ball of rock and metal. Its surface, or crust, is made of rock. On top of the crust lie the oceans and dry land. The oceans cover nearly three-quarters of Earth's surface. They help to keep Earth from getting too hot or too cold. During warm weather, the oceans soak up heat from the sun. Then, during colder weather, they give off heat and warm the air.

Underneath Earth's crust is a layer of heated rock called the mantle. This layer is about 1,800 miles (2,900 kilometers) thick. Beneath the mantle is the center of Earth, or its core. The core is probably made of iron and nickel and is terribly hot. Its temperature is about 11,000 degrees F. (6,000 degrees C.).

Earth has a blanket of air around it called the atmosphere. The atmosphere protects us from harmful rays given off by the sun. And, like the oceans, it helps to keep Earth from getting too hot or too cold.

Earth's atmosphere has many layers. Near the ground, the layers of air are thick and heavy. Higher in the sky, the layers of air get thinner. Finally, the air gets so thin that it disappears completely. This chart shows the five layers of the atmosphere and the layers inside of Earth.

Earth travels around the sun in about 365 days, or one year. As it travels, it is tilted to one side. Because of the way it tilts, half of Earth has summer while the other half has winter.

When the northern half of Earth is tilted toward the sun, that half has summer. When it is tilted away from the sun, the northern half has winter. At the same time the northern half is having winter, the southern half of Earth has summer. As the year goes by, different parts of Earth warm up and then cool off. The seasons change.

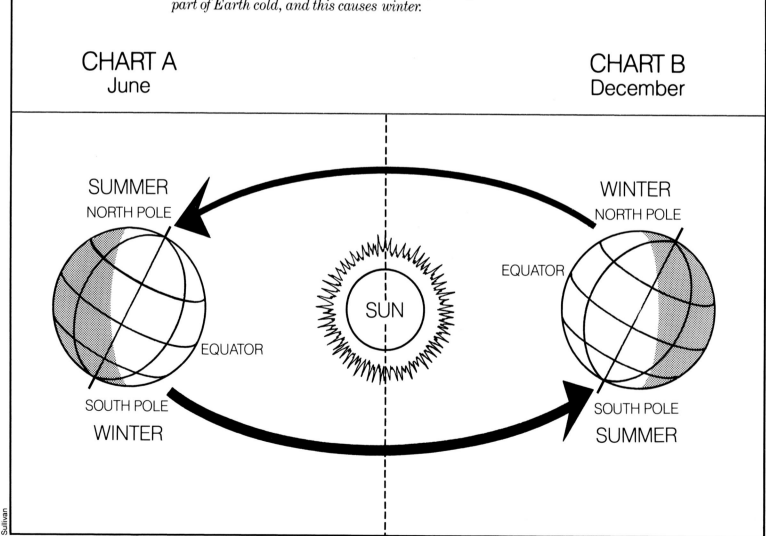

Chart A shows the northern half of Earth in June, when it is tilted toward the sun. Earth's northern half gets lots of sunlight in June, which makes it warm. This warmth causes summer. Chart B shows the northern half of Earth in December, when it is tilted away from the sun. It gets less sunlight at this time. The lack of sunlight makes that part of Earth cold, and this causes winter.

CHART A
June

CHART B
December

SUMMER
NORTH POLE

EQUATOR

SUN

EQUATOR

SOUTH POLE
WINTER

WINTER
NORTH POLE

EQUATOR

SOUTH POLE
SUMMER

Sullivan

7:30 A.M.

10:30 A.M.

NOON

These photographs show part of Earth as it turns into the sun's light and then turns away from the light into darkness. This movement of Earth causes our day and night. The photographs were taken from a satellite in orbit about 22,000 miles above South America.

7:30 P.M.

3:30 P.M.

Half of Earth always faces the sun and is covered with sunlight. The other half is always turned away from the sun and is covered with darkness. But Earth is constantly spinning on its axis. Each complete spin lasts one day, or 24 hours. As Earth spins, everything on it moves from sunlight into darkness, and back to sunlight once more. These periods of sunlight and darkness make our day and night.

In many ways, Earth is a very ordinary member of the solar system. It's not the biggest or the smallest planet. It's not the hottest or coldest or most beautiful planet, either. But for us, Earth is a very special place. Earth is our home.

Earth's Moon

Our next stop is the moon, Earth's closest neighbor. The moon is only 239,000 miles (384,000 kilometers) from Earth. It is much closer to us than the sun or the other planets.

The moon travels around Earth in the same way the planets move around the sun. The pull of Earth's gravity keeps the moon from flying off into space. Any object that travels around a planet in this way is called a satellite.

The moon is about one-fourth the size of Earth. Because it is so small, its gravity is too weak to hold an atmosphere. Without an atmosphere to protect it, the side of the moon facing the sun gets terribly hot. The side of the moon turned away from the sun gets colder than any place on Earth.

Besides Earth, the moon is the only other world that people have actually walked on. When astronauts landed on the moon, they found large, flat plains covered with rocks and dust. They also found tall mountains and billions of holes called craters. But they did not find water, air, or any sign of life. There was only a dead, silent world.

When we look up at the full moon, we can usually see dark shadows on its surface. The shadows seem to form a face that some people call "the man in the moon." These dark areas are the flat plains on the moon's surface. People used to think these plains were filled with water, so they named them *maria*, or seas. Now we know they are really dry, dusty areas of land.

Apollo astronaut John W. Young leaps high from the surface of the moon. Young could leap much higher on the moon than he could on Earth because the moon's gravity is much weaker.

NASA

NASA

The moon travels around Earth every 27.3 days. As it travels, it seems to change its shape. This happens because we see different portions of the moon's lighted side as it moves around Earth. We call these different shapes the moon's phases.

While it travels around Earth, the moon spins slowly on its axis. It takes 27.3 days to complete one spin—the same time that it takes to travel around Earth. As a result, the moon always keeps the same face turned toward us.

For hundreds of years, people wondered what the far side of the moon looked like. Because one side of the moon always faces Earth, no one had ever seen its other side. Then, about 20 years ago, astronauts flew behind the moon and took pictures of its far side. Their pictures showed a surprise. The far side of the moon has almost no flat plains. The near side is almost covered with these plains, so scientists were surprised to find that the far side is so different.

The astronauts learned many new things on their trips to the moon. They found that the rocks on the moon are very old. The oldest moon rock that they found dates back 4.5 billion years! The astronauts also learned that people could live on the moon if they brought their own water, air, and food from Earth. Perhaps someday we will build a base on the moon. Scientists could use the base to do experiments and to observe other planets. People might even spend their vacations on the moon.

This photograph of the full moon shows the dark shadows, or maria, *on its surface.*

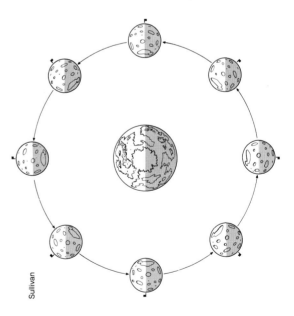

Sullivan

We can only see one side of the moon from Earth. As this chart shows, the moon's far side is never turned toward us.

Mars

Mars is only half the size of Earth. But in some ways, it is more like our home than any other planet in the solar system.

Earth has ice caps at the North and South Poles. So does Mars. The surface of the Earth is shaped by running water in streams and rivers. So is the surface of Mars. A day on Earth is 24 hours long. A day on Mars is only a half hour longer.

But Mars and Earth are very different worlds. Mars takes almost twice as long as Earth to circle the sun—687 Earth days. The air of Mars is too thin to breathe. Its rivers vanished long ago, and Mars is now a desert except for the ice caps. At high noon, temperatures can reach a comfortable 72 degrees F. (22 degrees C.), but at night the temperature drops as low as −271 degrees F. (−168 degrees C.).

The soil of Mars is rich in rust (iron oxide). That's why Mars looks red from space. From the surface of Mars, even the sky is pink, because of the rusty dust carried by the wind. Winds blow to great speeds on the surface, stirring up huge dust storms.

This photograph of Mars was taken from a powerful telescope on Earth.

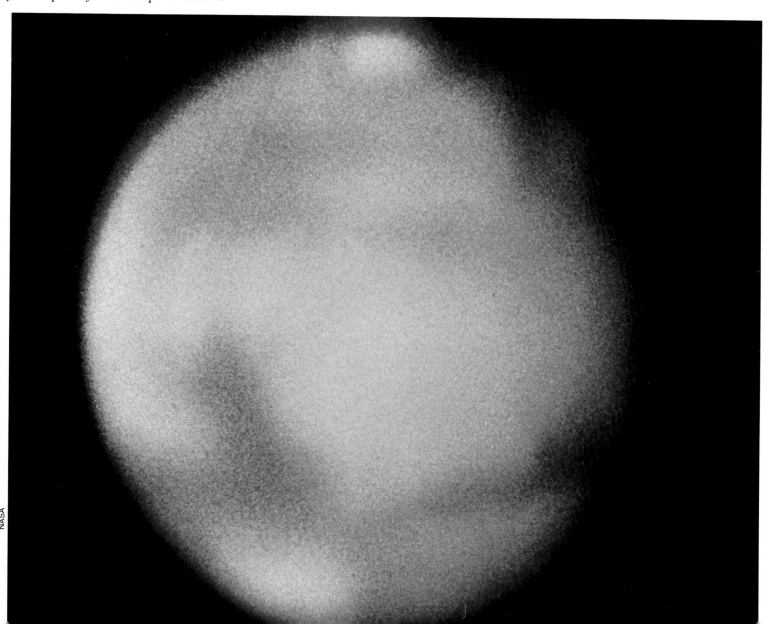

NASA

NASA

A sunset on Mars, as seen by the Viking spacecraft. The image has been improved by computer.

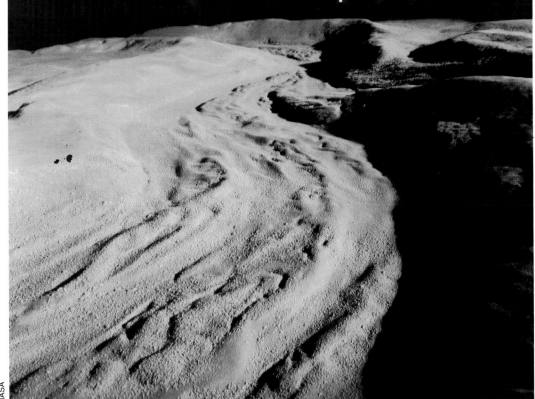

NASA

◀ In this painting of the red soil of Mars, we see the marks of water that flowed long ago. This dry channel would be about three miles wide.

NASA

*Mons Olympus, the mightiest
mountain in the solar system.*

Mars has two small, speedy moons. Phobos is the larger and faster
one. It zips around Mars in only 7½ hours. Deimos, the smaller, takes 30
hours to circle Mars.

Mars has huge mountains and deep canyons. Mons Olympus, a gigantic volcano, rises 16 miles (26 kilometers) into the Martian sky. It is three
times as high as Mount Everest. The Mariner Valley is over a mile deep and
2,800 miles (4,500 kilometers) long.

Scientists had the same hopes about Mars that they had about Venus. When people first looked at Mars through telescopes, they saw the dried-up rivers and thought they were canals. They believed that Martians might have built canals to carry water. They imagined huge, beautiful cities in the deserts, where Martians lived.

We got our first close look at Mars from the Viking spacecraft. These were robot spacecraft sent to Mars to tell us what it was like. The robots tested the air and soil of Mars and searched for signs of life—but found none. The canals turned out to be dry riverbeds. The deserts were empty. But a planet is a very big thing, and we have only searched a tiny part of it. Mars may hide more wonders than we can imagine.

The Viking robot spacecraft approaches Mars.

Asteroids

In this painting, two asteroids collide in the asteroid belt.

When we leave Mars behind, the solar system changes. Mars, Venus, and Mercury are like our Earth in many ways. Beyond Mars, though, the solar system is very different. The next few planets are giants, painted with colorful stripes like Easter eggs. At least three of these planets are circled by great rings.

Before we reach Jupiter—the first of the giant planets—we see thousands of little "dwarf" planets called asteroids. Asteroids are giant boulders and small chunks of rock, metal, and ice moving through space. Ceres, the largest asteroid, is over 600 miles (over 1,000 kilometers) wide. Other asteroids are the size of pebbles.

Most of the asteroids lie in the asteroid belt between Mars and Jupiter. A few—Eros, Apollo, and Amor—travel close to Earth and then swing far out among the giant planets.

Comets

Can you imagine a star with long hair? That's what a comet looks like in the sky. A comet is a big ball of frozen gas and rock—a "dirty snowball." Usually comets stay far out in space where we can't see them. But sometimes comets come in toward the sun. As they get near the sun, the frozen gas begins to melt. It streams behind them in a long tail that glows in the sun's light.

Long ago, when people saw the long tail of a comet stretch across the night sky, they were afraid. They thought that the comet was a sign of bad luck or of terrible things that would happen. When people saw comets through a telescope and learned about them, they stopped being afraid.

Some comets visit the solar system often. They circle the sun and head out into space again. Halley's Comet, discovered by Edmund Halley, passes Earth every 76 years on its way toward the sun. We will be able to see it at night in 1986.

Each time a comet travels toward the sun, a little more of it melts away. Finally there is hardly anything left at all—just dust and rocks speeding through space.

The comet Kahoutek appeared in our night sky in 1974.

Meteoroids

Comets are not the only strange streaks of light in the sky. There are also "shooting stars" that flash across the night like fiery spears.

People once thought that "shooting stars" were real stars that fell to Earth. Now we know that they are chunks of rock that have floated through space and entered Earth's atmosphere. These chunks of rock are called meteoroids. Some meteoroids are asteroids that wander out of the asteroid belt and fall to Earth. Others are leftover parts of comets that have melted away.

When a meteoroid falls to Earth, it falls at a terrible speed. It moves so fast that the air burns it. We see the burning rock as a streak of light flashing across the sky. The burning rock is called a meteor.

Most meteors burn up completely before they reach the ground. But the very largest meteors make it all the way to Earth—and leave giant holes in the ground where they strike. Once they reach the ground, we call them meteorites.

This huge hole, or crater, was made when a meteorite struck the earth in Arizona. The hole, which is called Meteor Crater, is 4,000 feet (1,200 meters) wide and 600 feet (185 meters) deep.

In each of these photographs, a small alphabet block is shown beside a meteorite. The alphabet blocks are all the same size, so they help you to compare the different sizes of the meteorites.

This meteorite, found in Antarctica, is made of rock very much like rocks found on Mars.

This meteorite, also from Antarctica, is made of rock much like the rocks found on our moon.

Meteorites come in many shapes and sizes. Most have been scarred by their fiery fall to Earth.

Jupiter

The Voyager spacecraft took this picture of Jupiter from 22 million miles (35.6 million kilometers) away.

The Great Red Spot amid the fantastic, swirling colors of Jupiter.

The fifth planet is the biggest planet in the solar system. Jupiter was named for the king of the Roman gods, and it is the "king" of all the planets. You can see it easily in the night sky. It shines more brightly than any other planet except Venus.

Jupiter is 1,300 times the size of Earth. It takes nearly 12 Earth years for mighty Jupiter to circle the sun. Yet the huge planet spins more than twice as fast as Earth.

Strangest of all, Jupiter has no surface, no ground to stand on. Jupiter is a giant ball of gas, a cloud squeezed tight; a smaller, cooler version of the sun. We call planets like Jupiter "gas giants." The tops of its clouds are terribly cold, but in the center, we think it may be 53,000 degrees F. (30,000 degrees C.).

Jupiter is a planet of storms. The clouds of Jupiter never stop swirling and changing shape. We can see lightning flash in them.

Yet there is one place on Jupiter that hardly changes. We call it the Great Red Spot, and it has been there for as long as we have looked closely at Jupiter. Most scientists think that the Great Red Spot is a storm of such great size that it could swallow three Earths.

*A volcano erupts on the surface
of Io in this computer-aided
photograph.*

The pictures of Jupiter were taken by Voyager, another robot space-craft. Jupiter is very far away, and Voyager gave us the first close look at the king of the planets.

Jupiter has moons, too—lots of them. Io, Europa, Ganymede, and Callisto are the largest, but we think there are 12 others.

Io looks like a pizza—all red, yellow, and white. Io has the solar system's only active volcanoes, aside from the ones on Earth. The volcanoes threw material from deep inside the moon across its surface, making Io's bright colors.

Europa is covered with cracked ice. (Ice is common out in this part of the solar system, far from the hot sun.) Callisto and Ganymede are both made of ice as well as rock. They look something like Earth's moon, though Ganymede is bigger. Ganymede is the biggest moon in the solar system.

Mighty Jupiter has a ring around it. It is made of dust and is very narrow and dark. You cannot see it from Earth. We did not even know the ring was there until we sent the Voyager robot to look at Jupiter. Voyager took pictures of the ring, glowing in the light of the distant sun, as the robot spacecraft headed outward toward the next planet in the solar system.

Four of Jupiter's moons are shown in this photograph. Io is on the upper left. Europa is on the upper right. Below them are Ganymede on the left and Callisto on the right.

NASA

Saturn

This photograph of Saturn was taken from Earth through a telescope.

Long ago, a man named Galileo aimed a telescope at the sky and saw a planet that looked like it had ears. The planet was a bright spot in the sky, and he saw two small blobs of light sticking out from opposite sides of it.

Later, other people with better telescopes got the first clear view of the planet. They saw that the "ears" were rings circling a golden world. We learned only a little while ago that Jupiter has a ring. But Saturn—the sixth planet—has been called "the ringed planet" for a long time. The lovely, mysterious rings are the first thing you notice when you look at Saturn.

NASA

Saturn is another gas giant, a ball of colored gas. It is almost 800 times the size of Earth. It takes nearly 30 Earth years to circle the sun, but only 10 hours and 14 minutes to turn once on its axis. The tops of its golden clouds are terribly cold and its center is terribly hot.

The rings look solid, but they are not. They are really made of thousands and thousands of pieces of ice and rock circling Saturn like tiny moons. But there are so many of them so close together that, from a distance, they look like solid rings. The Voyager spacecraft visited Saturn and sent us the beautiful picture of the rings shown below.

A computer added these bright colors to the beautiful rings of Saturn. This picture was taken by Voyager from nearly nine million miles away.

NASA

Saturn and its moons. This picture was made from many separate photographs taken by Voyager.

Saturn has at least 22 moons—the most of any planet in the solar system. Its largest moon is Titan. This moon is the only one in the solar system that has its own air, though it is not air you could breathe. Saturn's other large moons include Enceladus, Tethys, Dione, Rhea, and Iapetus.

Saturn is the last planet in the solar system that we know well. Our spacecraft have not visited the other planets yet, though they will in the future. And we can barely see the other planets from Earth, because they are so far away.

These are the largest moons of the solar system. Titan is a moon of Saturn. Io, Europa, Ganymede, and Callisto belong to Jupiter. We call Earth's moon simply "the moon."

If you journeyed into Saturn's atmosphere and looked up at the sky, this is what you might see. The rings shine brightly in a cloud-filled sky.

Uranus

This painting shows the dark rings of Uranus, which were discovered in 1977.

Dixon

Sullivan

This is how Uranus might look if you stood on one of its moons.

The axis of Earth is slightly tilted as it circles the sun. But the axis of Uranus lies far over on one side.

Because it is so far away, Uranus is a place of mystery. In Earth's night sky, it looks like a faint star. You can find it only if you know just where to look.

We know that Uranus is a gas giant almost 300 times the size of Earth. It is the seventh planet in the solar system, and it is greenish-blue in color. The tops of its clouds are terribly cold, but its center is very hot.

Like other gas giants, it has rings—nine of them, circling the planet like thin, dark hoops. Scientists believe the rings are made of dark dust. Uranus also has five small moons. They show only as tiny bright dots even in the world's most powerful telescopes.

The strangest thing about Uranus is the way it circles the sun. It takes 84 Earth years to move around the sun, and only 16 hours to turn once on its axis. But, instead of standing straight up-and-down in space, Uranus lies on its side. As it spins, it circles the sun like a rolling ball.

Neptune

NASA

Mysterious Neptune with its moon, Triton, seen against the background of stars.

The last gas giant in the solar system is Neptune, the eighth planet. It is about the same size as Uranus, nearly 300 times larger than Earth. It is pale blue in color. We know that it is hot inside. Neptune gives off more heat than it gets from the distant sun. Neptune takes 164 Earth years to circle the sun, and it turns once on its axis in 16 to 18 hours.

You cannot see Neptune at all in the night sky, unless you look through a telescope. Scientists searched the night sky for years before they found the dim pinpoint that was Neptune.

We have not been able to see any rings around Neptune yet. There may or may not be rings there. We will not be sure until we send robot spacecraft for a closer look. We do know that Neptune has two moons. Triton is bigger than our moon, and Nereid is much smaller.

We call Neptune the eighth planet, but right now it's really the planet farthest from the sun. Why? Because another planet—the last and coldest in the solar system—has moved closer to the sun than Neptune.

Pluto

Pluto, the ninth planet, is a hard, frozen snowball circling the sun. It is so far away that, if you were on Pluto, the sun would look like only a very bright star. Pluto, which has one moon called Charon, is the coldest place in the entire solar system.

Pluto is a little smaller than Earth's moon. In fact, many people think it was once a moon of Neptune that wandered away from its planet. Other people think that Pluto fell into the solar system from outer space and began circling the sun. It is certainly nothing like the gas giant planets that rule the outer edges of the solar system.

Pluto circles the sun in a strange way. Sometimes it swings far out into space. At other times, it moves closer to the sun. Until the year 1999, Pluto will actually be closer to the sun than Neptune.

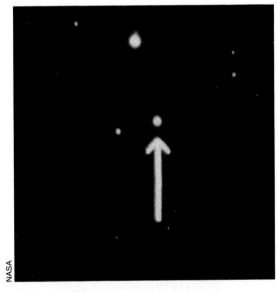

Seen from Earth, Pluto is only a dim spot, even through the biggest telescopes.

◀ *In this painting, we see Pluto and its moon, Charon, far from the warming sun.*

The Stars of Space

And beyond Pluto, what is there?

Darkness. Emptiness. Terrible cold. Distances greater than you can imagine. And at the end of those great distances are the stars, each a mighty, blazing sun.

Stars come in many sizes and colors. Our sun is a medium-size yellow star. There are red stars and blue stars and white stars, giant stars and supergiants and dwarf stars. Sometimes two stars blaze close together, circling each other like bright dancers in space. And sometimes stars explode, hurling their unbelievable energy into space. When stars explode, they may leave a giant cloud of gas and dust behind. These giant clouds are called nebulas.

Some of the stars may have planets circling them. We cannot tell because the stars are so far away. There may be living beings like ourselves there, looking upward at the night sky and wondering what kind of people live on other planets circling other stars.

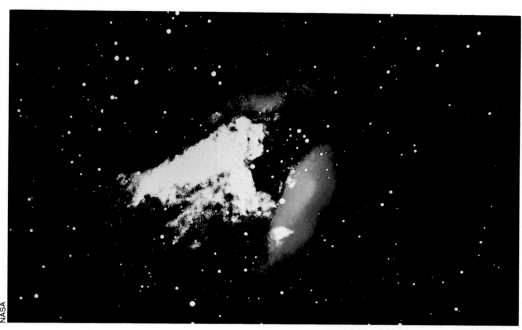

NASA

The Orion Nebula, an immense glowing cloud of gas and dust among the distant stars.

This spiral galaxy is a gathering ▶ place of stars. Our solar system is part of another spiral galaxy, which we call the Milky Way.

This nebula looks like a bird spreading its wings. It is called the Swan Nebula. The bright colors in this picture were added by a computer.

NASA